BOB IGER BOOK

The Life Story of Robert Allen Iger

GILBERT BUCKLEY

CONTENTS

INTRODUCTION

Being one of a kind in business, there exists a rationale for Robert A. Iger's continued status as one of the most esteemed chief executive officers globally.

This is the story of the Disney Boss — a man who has successfully overseen great acquisitions, supported the creation of influential films that shape societal norms, introduced pioneering methods of distribution, and achieved commendable financial outcomes in the business world. Throughout these paths, he has consistently demonstrated a steadfast commitment to acknowledging the indispensable contributions of both employees and fans, who have played a pivotal role in facilitating these achievements.

The reappointment of Iger as Chief Executive Officer in 2022 marked the beginning of a distinct period characterized by significant changes and a heightened focus on innovative achievements for the preeminent corporation renowned for its enchanting offerings. He distinguishes himself via his genuineness and practicality. Iger thinks that genuine power and effective leadership stem from an individual's self-awareness and authenticity, rather than assuming a false persona. Iger has acquired a significant amount of knowledge and personal growth as a result of his leadership experiences worth knowing and learning from.

Today, Robert Iger is one of the most well-known names in business in the United States. But what makes him stand out for us?

We know Iger as the brain behind many of Disney's wins. But beyond the bright and complicated world of entertainment, there is an interesting story of commitment, kindness, and steadfast support for causes bigger than oneself.

Iger has a big impact on many places, from the busy streets of Los Angeles to the holy halls of the University of Chicago, from the happy laughter of kids at Disneyland to the serious promises made to important causes like the Obama Foundation. His charitable work, which he often does with his wife, Willow Bay, shows that he and she both want to live in a world where success isn't just measured by personal gains but also by the good things that people do after they die.

With this book, we get a glimpse of a time when business and kindness come together to make rollers of change and hope as we learn about the important things Iger and the people in his group have done. It's an account of good leadership, having a vision, and always working to make tomorrow better. Come with us as we untie Robert Iger's life story!

THE EARLY YEARS OF ROBERT IGER

Growing Up

Robert Allen Iger's story is that of a Jewish family living in the busy city of New York. Born to Miriam "Mimi" and Arthur L. Iger, he was their first child.

Arthur, Robert's dad, was a very interesting person in his own way. He had a great history as a Navy warrior who served during the rough times of World War II. He had important jobs after the war, like senior vice president and general manager at the Greenvale Marketing Corporation. He was good at more than just business. As an advertising and public relations professor, he shared his knowledge with others. Arthur had many skills, including playing the trumpet very well, even though he was dealing with the difficulties of having manic-depressive disorder.

On the other hand, Robert's mother made a name for herself at Boardman Junior High School in Oceanside, New York, which is on the other side of the family.

Joe, Robert's grandpa on his dad's side, was also not an average personality. He was related to the famous cartoonist Jerry Iger, whose name was heard all over the art world.

As a child, Robert Iger lived in Oceanside, a friendly neighborhood, and started his schooling there. First, he went to Fulton Avenue School. Eventually, his road took him to Oceanside High School, where he finished with honors in 1969.

It wasn't enough for Robert to want to learn, though. He went to college with a strong desire to learn. He learned everything he knew about TV and radio at the Roy H. Park School of Communications at Ithaca College and passed with good colors. Because he worked hard and did well, he was given the honorific title magna cum laude, which shows how smart he was. In 1973, he successfully completed his undergraduate studies and was awarded a Bachelor of Science degree. This was the start of an amazing path that would eventually change his future in entertainment.

THE PROGRESSION OF IGER'S CAREER

It was in 1972 that Iger began his long and successful career in the media world. Everything started at Ithaca College, where he assumed the role of host for the TV show "Campus Probe." Iger did a lot of different things over the course of five months. He wanted to be a famous news reporter, but he also showed how versatile he was by being a weatherman in Ithaca. But as time went on, Iger's work goals changed, giving him a glimpse of the endless opportunities that lay ahead.

A Tenure at the ABC

This is how Bob Iger's long and successful career with the American Broadcasting Company (ABC) began in 1974. In his early years, he worked as a nanny and learned the intricate details of TV production for a meager $150 a week. When you take inflation into account, this is about $700 today.

In 1988, a very important year, Iger was in charge of the Calgary Winter Olympics as the top program leader. But these Games had to deal with the unpredictable state of nature; bad weather and the delays that came with it were big problems. To get around these problems and keep to their show schedule, Iger and his skilled team found interesting human interest stories to include in the news. People fell in love with stories like the one about the cute Jamaican sledding team and Eddie the Eagle's unbreakable spirit. ABC's numbers went through the roof after this masterful piece of writing. People took notice of how calm Iger was during the storm. Daniel Burke and Thomas Murphy, two powerful people at ABC, saw how talented he was and helped him move up at the company.

By 1989, Iger had more power because he was in charge of ABC Entertainment. Famous TV shows like "Twin Peaks," "America's Funniest Home Videos," and the experimental "Cop Rock" were made possible by him. After that, he was put in charge of the ABC Network Television Group as president in January 1993. After only a few months, in March, he was promoted to senior vice president for Capital Cities/ABC. But his quick rise didn't end there. By July of that same year, he was named executive vice president.

The next year, was the peak of Bob Iger's career when, in 1994, he was named president and chief operating officer of Capital Cities/ABC, the respected parent company that ran ABC.

IGER'S LEADERSHIP AT DISNEY: MAJOR MILESTONES AND ROLE SHIFTS

Disney's Media World Transformation

In 1995, something big happened in the media world: The Walt Disney Company bought Capital Cities/ABC and changed its name to ABC, Inc. During this time of change, Iger took on the job of chairman with ease, which he did until 1999.

On February 25, 1999, a big turn was made in the story of Iger's rise. On this day, he was given the job of president of Walt Disney International, which meant he was in charge of all of Disney's businesses around the world. In addition to this, he was appointed as the leader of the ABC Group. This important move changed his focus and took him away from the day-to-day details of ABC. Disney saw this change as an opportunity to promote the busy executive.

Later, a new role came Iger's way with the start of the new century. Disney made him president and Chief Operating Officer (COO) on January 24, 2000. This made him the second-in-command and put him directly under the watchful eye of Michael Eisner, chairman and CEO. It's important to note that Disney didn't have a clear head until Eisner took over after Michael Ovitz's 16-month stint.

Board Politics & CEO Succession

The winds of change blew again through Disney in the year 2005. Roy E. Disney and Stanley Gold, two board members, led the "Save Disney" movement, which was mostly an attempt to overthrow Eisner's rule. It was now time to look for someone to take over as CEO after Eisner. Iger quickly became the center of attention, and on March 13, 2005, Disney named him the clear heir to Eisner's throne. So, Iger became the practical leader, while Eisner kept the title of "CEO" until he retired on September 30, 2005.

In July 2005, the rough days calmed down when Disney and Gold dropped their effort to work with Iger instead. Iger made some important choices in his early years as CEO. He moved Disney's chief planner Peter Murphy to a different job and got rid of the company's Strategic Planning section. Aside from that, people started calling him "Bob" instead of "Robert" out of love.

Pixar Acquisition & Oswald's Return

One other important thing Bob Iger did was on January 24, 2006. Under his wise leadership, The Walt Disney Company announced plans to buy the groundbreaking Pixar Animation Studios for an amazing $7.4 billion, which will be paid for totally with stocks.

Iger also made a smart move that year when he took back Walt Disney's character Oswald the Lucky Rabbit from NBCUniversal by moving sportscaster Al Michaels from ABC to NBC Sports.

Marvel and the Power of Acquisition

Things changed in August 2009, when Iger was once again in charge. This time, he led the talks that led to Disney's historic $4 billion purchase of Marvel Entertainment and all of its brands. Later by 2014, this spending had paid off, as Marvel movies made huge amounts of money at the box office.

Board Affiliations & Lucasfilm Purchase

On October 7, 2011, Disney stated that Iger would become head of the board because John Pepper was leaving the board in March 2012. Also, Apple, Inc., led by CEO Tim Cook, added Iger to its board of directors on November 15, 2011, which was a big nod across industries. Through the early Pixar deal, Iger's power was a big part of making Steve Jobs Disney's biggest shareholder.

In October 2012, Iger made history when he arranged with the famous director George Lucas to buy Lucasfilm for a cool $4 billion. This deal opened the doors to the huge "Star Wars" world and gave Disney control of the famous "Indiana Jones" series.

Expansion to Shanghai & Job Creation Advocacy

Moving on to the theme park field, Iger announced the long-awaited opening date for the Shanghai Disney Resort in March 2016. This huge show, which cost $5.5 billion to build, was supposed to amaze people starting on June 16, 2016.

In May of that year, Iger wrote on Facebook that over the previous ten years, Disneyland had hired 11,000 new workers, and a staggering 18,000 more had joined other Disney businesses during that time. In a direct way, Iger asked Vermont Senator Bernie Sanders to explain himself by asking him about his work to create jobs.

Tenure Extensions & Leadership Commitment

In the beginning, Bob Iger was supposed to leave his role as Chairman and CEO of Disney on June 30, 2018. Still, things started to change when Disney officially announced in March 2017 that Iger would stay on as CEO until July 2, 2019. This was made even better by a deal for him to work as a consultant for the next three years. As proof of how important he is, Iger's term as CEO was extended again in December 2017, making it last until 2021.

The Fox Integration

In July 2018, Iger led a major change when owners from both Disney and 21st Century Fox approved a deal. With this smart move, in 2019, Disney was able to get important assets from Fox.

Phasing Out & Streaming Era

In April 2019, Iger announced that he would be stepping down as CEO and chairman of Disney by 2021. This was news that many people had been waiting for but hoped wouldn't come soon. Iger stepped down from Apple's board of directors in September 2019 to further avoid possible conflicts of interest. It was made at a time when both Disney and Apple were getting ready to start their streaming services, Disney+ and Apple TV+.

The Chapek Era and Pandemic Challenges

Iger said he was stepping down, and on February 25, 2020, Bob Chapek, who was head of Disney Parks, Experiences, and Products at the time, was announced as the new CEO. Iger didn't cut all links with the company; he became executive chairman, a position designed to oversee the change of power. But in a surprise move because of the problems caused by the COVID-19 pandemic, the board decided to keep Iger in charge and extend his contract until the end of 2021. In the last few months of the year, Iger gave Susan Arnold the job of chairman.

The Return of Iger & Unwavering Leadership

On November 20, 2022, Chapek was removed from his position by the Disney board, resulting in the reinstatement of Iger as the Chief Executive Officer. Upon his return to Disney, Iger initially consented to assume the position for a duration of two years, during which he would actively seek out a suitable candidate to succeed him. On July 12, 2023, Iger and Disney entered into an agreement to extend the contract duration to the conclusion of 2026.

WRITING CAREER

Robert Iger's autobiography, "The Ride of a Lifetime," came out in September 2019 and quickly shot to the top of the prestigious New York Times Best Seller list. As the story goes on, it follows Iger's career from its humble beginnings as a junior studio worker at ABC over the course of 45 years. Among the many stories he tells, Iger talks about how hard he worked to make the Shanghai Disneyland Park a reality, which took him to travel to China an amazing 40 times over the course of 18 years.

His book is a lesson in how to be a leader and have a goal. Iger paints a clear picture of the values and beliefs that drove every decision he made during the 15 years he led Disney, bringing one of the world's most beloved brands back to life and making it bigger. Some of the most touching parts of the book are his friendship with the late tech genius Steve Jobs and his deep respect for the stories behind Star Wars.

NPR said that "The Ride of a Lifetime" was one of the best books they read this year. Iger's message runs through all of its pages: that it is possible and even necessary to be kind and smart at the same time, choosing morality over pure profit. These kinds of rules aren't just for people in the workplace; they work for anyone who wants to be clear and sure of themselves at work and in their personal lives as well.

In "The Ride of a Lifetime," Iger distills the lessons he learned while heading over 220,000 employees as master of the Disney ship. He explains the basics of good leadership and shines a light on the qualities that make a real leader. One of these principles that Iger stresses is being positive. He thought that an upbeat leader could steer through rough seas by focusing on possible answers instead of dwelling on problems or pointing fingers.

KEY TAKEAWAYS FROM THE RIDE OF A LIFETIME

Major Acquisitions and Their Impact

Disney's life changed when it bought Pixar, Marvel, Lucasfilm, and 21st Century Fox. Iger gets involved in every part of every deal, from the first talks to the final discussions. He talks about the problems that had to be solved, like persuading the Disney board, talking with Steve Jobs

(Pixar), and making sure that these companies would fit in with Disney's culture.

Challenges and Crises

There were some tough times during Iger's time in office. He talks about how to run a business during economic downturns, how to handle issues, and how to handle sudden problems. The tragedy at Pulse nightclub and the alligator situation at a Disney resort were especially hard times. Iger thinks about how important it is to be a caring leader during these times.

Innovations and Forward Thinking

Disney welcomed new technologies while Iger was in charge. He talks about the start of Disney+, the company's streaming service, and the difficulties of competing with big companies like Netflix in the digital world.

Personal Stories and Thoughts

Iger talks about personal events that have shaped the way he leads. He talks about his father's impact on him, the role of teachers like Roone Arledge and Tom Murphy, and his meetings with famous people in the business, such as George Lucas and Rupert Murdoch

Leadership Philosophy

Iger is known for being cool, having good business sense, and putting a lot of value on brands. In the book, he talks about the principles of his leadership style. He stresses how important it is, to be honest, have the guts to take measured risks, and create an environment where creativity and innovation can grow.

"The Ride of a Lifetime," is a great way to learn about the ideas that have shaped his life over the years. In short, it is a great book for learning how to be a leader, make plans, and negotiate. It gives a unique look into the business world, the world of entertainment, and the life of one of the most important people in the industry.

Courage: Iger says that courage isn't just facing danger; it's also being brave enough to take measured chances and make big investments. Being bold and not worrying about failing is what drives people to come up with new ideas.

Decisiveness: You can't put off making decisions forever, especially hard ones. Iger stresses how important it is to make decisions quickly. Not making a choice for a long time not only wastes time and money but can also seriously hurt team spirit.

Fairness: For Iger, leadership is about more than just the mind. It's also about the heart. Fair treatment based on kindness and understanding must go hand in hand with an open-door strategy that makes sure everyone on the team can reach you.

There's more to "The Ride of a Lifetime" than just a job story in it. It shows how important it is to have a goal, keep going, and be a leader. Iger's rise from a boy from a small town to the head of one of the biggest entertainment companies in the world is an example. Among other things,

he stresses how important it is to stay true

to your ideals, be flexible when things

change, and work hard.

AWARDS AND AFFILIATIONS

Bob Iger has been praised over the years for more than just his work as CEO of The Walt Disney Company. He is also known for having a big impact on the world of media and for his diplomatic work. Robert Iger's journey, which is full of awards and praise, shows how to be a leader who combines vision, kindness, and drive in a way that works well. Here is a list of some of his most important awards and connections, in no order:

✓ Fortune magazine named them one of the "25 Most Powerful People in

Business" for two years in a row, from 2006 to 2007.

✓ Given the "CEO of the Year" award by both MarketWatch in 2006 and Chief Executive magazine in 2014.

✓ Institutional Investor magazine named him one of its "Best CEOs" every year from 2008 to 2011.

✓ Iger is also a well-known tech figure. From 2011 to 2019, he served on the board of Apple Inc.

✓ In 2012, he was inducted into the prestigious Academy of Motion

Picture Arts and Sciences. This is an organization that recognizes and honors excellent accomplishments in many areas, such as education, the arts, public service, and charity work. Iger didn't just take the award lying down; he also became head of the capital campaign for the Academy Museum of Motion Pictures in Los Angeles, which is about to open.

✓ Inducted into the Programming and Cable Hall of Fame, which shows how important he is to the field of programming.

✓ Forbes magazine named them one of the "World's Most Powerful People" in 2019.

✓ named TIME's Businessperson of the Year, which shows how smart and effective he is as a boss.

✓ In 2020, Iger had two reasons to celebrate: he was admitted into both the Television Hall of Fame and the Television Academy Hall of Fame. The awards he has received show how much he has influenced and improved television as a medium.

✓ In 2022, the late Queen Elizabeth II made him an Honorary Knight Commander of the Most Excellent Order of the British Empire. This was a very important honor for him. The award wasn't just for his personal accomplishments; it was also a nod to his part in improving international ties between the UK and the USA.

ROBERT IGER'S PERSONAL LIFE

Marital Life

In the huge business and success stories, we rarely see the quiet lines of love and friendship that often support and maintain these well-known people. Robert Iger is one of the biggest names in the entertainment business, and his story is deeply connected to that of Willow Bay, his wife of more than 24 years.

Robert Iger and Willow Bay have been married since 1995, which is the start of a relationship that has stood the test of time. This wasn't Iger's first marriage; he was married to Kathleen Susan Iger before this one, and they had two children together, Amanda and Kate. They did, however, end their marriage in 1994, and Iger found love and friendship again with Bay the next year.

With Bay, their family got bigger when their two kids, Robert and William, were born. For Iger and Bay, the best parts of life have always been the times they spent with their kids. Even though they both have busy jobs, these private family times are what their relationship is all about.

About Willow Bay

Willow Bay started her working life out of the blue. She didn't start out as a model because she wanted to; she did it by accident when she asked "Seventeen Magazine" for a job. When she was seen as more of a possible model than an intern, her career took a turn for the better, and she signed with Ford Models. Because of her work as a model, including her time with Estee Lauder, she was able to finally become a journalist. Bay's career path has been nothing short of amazing, from leading CNN's Moneyline to holding a number of reporting roles.

Years ago, Willow Bay added another feather to her cap by going to school. In 2017, she was given the honor of being named Dean of the Annenberg School for Communication and Journalism at USC. This made history at the school because she was the first woman to hold this position.

In a frank 2020 interview with Iger, Bay talked about their journey together and said that they met on June 13, 1994, which was the day they fell in love. The things they've done together over the years, like taking care of the house or watching their favorite TV shows, show how close they are.

People who follow Bay online mostly see her work-related posts, but she doesn't mind sharing personal moments with her fans every once in a while. Her social media gives people a look into her life, whether she's sharing a real moment with Iger on the way to the Oscars or showing bits of her trips and events.

People usually think of Robert Iger's business successes when they think of him, but it's important to remember the love and support that have been with him along the way. With her many jobs and projects she works on with Iger, Willow Bay is a great example of love, commitment, and success in her own way.

Bob Iger in 2023: The Health Rumors

Recently, there were a lot of rumors going around online about how healthy Disney's famous CEO, Bob Iger, is. Disney fans and people in general are becoming more and more worried about his safety.

While there are a lot of claims about Iger's health, it's important to tell the difference between speculation and fact. The fast spread of these untrue stories has created a cloud of doubt, which has made the conversation more difficult and fed the gossip mill even more. This has led to different reactions from people close to Bob Iger to these reports. For many, just the idea that his health might be getting worse has made them feel sad and worried.

Nonetheless, the unexpected 2022 news that Bob Iger was stepping down as CEO of Disney made rumors even stronger. A lot of people quickly connected this choice to possible health problems. Some sources said that Bob Iger might be dealing with the manic-depressive condition, which was one of the ideas. It is very important to stress that these claims have not been backed up by any solid proof yet, so people should be very careful when making conclusions. On the other hand, a closer look at the situation, though, would reveal a different story: Iger's choice was based on the end of his contract, which disproved a major theory. His 2023 return to leadership is a testament to this.

Altogether, in a time when information is instantly shared, it's important to be careful and calm when talking about such sensitive subjects. It's important to stay away from unproven rumors about Bob Iger's health and choices until official comments or facts come out.

Politics

Bob Iger, with his vast influence and role at the helm of one of the world's most significant media conglomerates, has naturally been a figure of interest in the political landscape. His self-identification as a political centrist might come as a surprise to some, especially given the polarized nature of contemporary politics.

Iger's political journey has seen him move across party lines. His earlier association with the Democratic Party indicates that he was, at least at one point, in alignment with their values and platforms. This alignment, however, seems to have wavered in 2016, a notably tumultuous year in American politics. Switching to independent status can often be seen as a desire to distance oneself from the rigidity of party politics and maintain flexibility in one's political decisions.

His public clash with Bernie Sanders over labor issues at Disney Resort gives insight into the real-world implications of corporate decisions and their intersection with politics. Sanders, a known advocate for workers' rights and higher minimum wages, seemed to be a natural critic of practices at Disney Resort. Iger's decision to address Sanders directly on Facebook is indicative of how business leaders today are more direct and public in their political communications, especially given the vast reach and immediate nature of social media platforms.

Iger's involvement in fundraising for Hillary Clinton's presidential campaign further solidifies his leanings towards the Democratic side of the spectrum, at least in that electoral cycle. However, his subsequent appointment to President-elect Trump's Strategic and Policy Forum demonstrates a willingness to work across the aisle and engage with different political ideologies. This cross-party collaboration, however, was not without its limits. Iger's resignation from the Forum, following Trump's controversial decision to pull out of the Paris Climate Agreement, reveals a point of contention and a line that Iger was unwilling to cross.

Iger's political engagements over the years, spanning different parties and presidents, underscores the minutiae and convolutions inherent in the politics of a business leader of his stature. It also raises questions about the role and responsibility of corporate leaders in today's political climate. Should they remain neutral, or is there an expectation for them to take stand on pressing global issues?

AN OUTLINE OF CONTROVERSIES STOKED BY ROBERT IGER OVER THE COURSE OF HIS CAREER

The idea that Disney was pushing a "woke agenda" or going against Walt Disney's core values was one of the big problems Iger had to deal with. This feeling got stronger because of how Disney handled the Parental Rights in Education Bill, its legal battle with Ron DeSantis that led to Disney suing the Florida Governor, and the chaos surrounding the Reedy Creek Improvement District, which is now known as the Central Florida Tourism Oversight District. What did Iger say about these things? Here is a collection of his

Controversial points of view that has been put together.

Disney's Vision for Inclusive Entertainment

At the 2023 Disney Shareholder Meeting, someone spoke very well about how they saw what they saw as a growing focus on progressive social beliefs (often called the "woke agenda") in Disney's movies. Additionally, they said that the prestigious company might have worked on purpose with people who had been previously linked to shady behavior, especially in order to make songs for a younger audience. Also, the speaker asked with emotion and belief a question that made us think: would Disney think about not talking about LGBTQIA+ and gender issues in their content? They wanted to go back in time to a time when Disney was mostly seen as a safe place to have fun. They thought that Disney could rebuild its relationship with families and gain the trust of investors again by taking such a step.

People with these strong views might be interested in Iger's answer. When asked about these points, Mr. Iger answered with kindness and clarity, stressing that Disney is fully committed to being open to everyone and wants to be a place where everyone feels welcome. Iger told the crowd that Disney's main goal is to entertain, even though he admitted that some reviewers see Disney's material as pushing a certain story. According to him, the main goal should always be to tell interesting stories instead of trying to get a point across.

It was still unclear what Iger's position would mean for Disney's future content creation, but it was clear from his answer that Disney's main goal is to tell stories for fun, not to promote any particular philosophy.

Parental Concerns: A Commitment to Diverse Storytelling at the 2023 Shareholder Meeting

Iger went into more detail as the talk went on, especially when it came to parents' worries about the kind of information their kids could access. He admitted that making content that appeals to everyone is hard and that Disney can't always get everyone to like something. Nevertheless, he stressed an important point: parents have different levels of safety when it comes to their kids' television exposure.

Iger said that he really wanted parents to trust and feel safe in Disney's products in a sincere way. He talked about how Disney is always working to find content that appeals to a wide range of age groups in a family setting. Iger stressed that Disney's goal is to tell stories that represent the complex web of our global society, going beyond just pleasure. Disney hopes that these kinds of stories will help people of all ages understand things better, see things from different points of view, and be more open to others.

Some people think that Iger's opinion on Disney's future content will have effects in the future, but his wise comments about parents' different levels of comfort with their kids' media intake made people think a lot.

Disney's Vision and the Floridian Project

In the long history of Disney, Bob Iger has been a key figure. He has often talked about the reasons behind Disney's huge project in Florida. In a conversation with TIME Magazine, Iger talked about Walt Disney's goal of changing the world. Tens of thousands were hired because of the big project, which turned Central Florida's once-desolate swamplands into a booming economic force. Under Disney's leadership, the area grew into one of the most popular vacation destinations in the United States, drawing millions of visitors every year. Without a doubt, this project has been good for both Disney and the state of Florida.

For Iger, the main reason for taking on such a big project was clear. He saw Disney's role in Florida going in two different directions: first, to consistently increase value for both its customers and the state; and second, to build a mutually beneficial relationship with Florida that would make it easier for Disney to do business there.

Iger on Disney's Controversy in Florida: The Interplay of Free Speech and Politics at the 2023 Shareholder Meeting

People who followed what was happening in Florida noticed a strong connection between Disney's strong opposition to the Parental Rights in Education Bill, also known as the "Don't Say Gay" bill, and what Governor DeSantis and the state legislature did next. In the years that followed, the Reedy Creek District changed a lot, and Disney's control over its areas became much less noticeable.

At the 2023 annual meeting of shareholders, Bob Iger talked about this issue straight on. Even though he agreed with Disney's position on the controversial Florida law, he also said that the company may not have properly communicated its position. On the other hand, he passionately supported the idea that companies, like people, have the right to use their freedom of speech.

Iger didn't hold back when he said that Governor DeSantis's clear unhappiness with Disney's position seemed to have led to retaliatory actions, such as the creation of a new oversight board to keep an eye on Disney's many assets and operations. Iger's feelings were a reflection of a deep-seated worry: the possible punishing undertones of such a move, which seemed meant to scold Disney for using its constitutional rights.

Some people tried to paint a more complex picture of what happened, but Iger's honesty was clear. He didn't hold back when he accused Governor DeSantis of punishing Disney for practicing its legally protected freedom. The fight between the two giants didn't seem to be going away, which meant that things would get even more rough in the future.

At the 2023 shareholders' meeting, Bob Iger spoke from the heart about his love for Florida, also known as the "Sunshine State." His respect was clear, and it showed not only in words but also in actions, like giving money for 50 years and doing many other things to help the community. Iger made a picture of how committed Disney is to the state's well-being, from creating jobs to supporting tourists and from doing community service to paying taxes on time.

Iger talked about the main issue, which seemed to be the punishments given to Disney, in a serious way. The main point of his case was that he thought it was unfair to punish a business or person for simply exercising their civil rights. He said this was especially true when the company being attacked had been a strong supporter of the state. The impressive number of over 75,000 people who work at Disney is a clear example of this.

Iger talked about how about 50 million people were expected to visit Disney's sites that year, with about 8 million of them coming from outside of the United States. This made Disney's impact even bigger. When it came to money, he was happy to say that Disney paid a lot of taxes in the state.

But Iger's speech wasn't just about the past; he also talked about big plans for the future, promising that up to 17 billion dollars would be spent on Walt Disney World over the next ten years. These plans for the future said they would create about 13,000 new jobs at Disney and a huge number of other jobs in secondary ways. Investing in this way would always lead to more tourists, which would bring in more tax money.

At the end of his passionate speech, Iger repeated a worry. Stopping a business from moving forward just to argue against its constitutional stance seemed short-sighted and bad for Florida's interests as a whole, not just Disney's. Such strong words spoken during a storm of conflict showed how complicated the relationships between corporations, the law, and the state are.

Getting Through Tough Times

There were, however, some other problems during Iger's time as CEO. There was bad news about Disney's top leaders in a 2019 Vanity Fair article. Actress Paz de la Huerta sued Harvey Weinstein, alleging that both Iger and former CEO Michael Eisner made a sequence of decisions that facilitated a variety of actions by Weinstein, resulting in unacceptable harm to specific employees. Disney stood firm and said they had no knowledge of any of these actions happening while Weinstein was working at Miramax Films.

A 2017 story in Variety said that Iger may have known about a disturbing event that happened at an Oscar party in 2010. It was said that Pixar's John Lasseter was acting inappropriately with a young employee during the episode. These claims seemed to be similar to earlier, unnamed claims about Lasseter's behavior that were said to have been known to the top leaders of the company since the 1990s.

The Unions and Clashing

Bob Iger's journey with Disney is a mix of successes and disagreements that shows how hard it is to run a global entertainment giant. Around 2023, there was another event that made Iger famous. Iger talked about his worries and dislike of the strikes started by the Writers Guild of America (WGA) and the Screen Actors Guild-American Federation of Television and Radio Artists (SAG-AFTRA) on CNBC. He said that their actions were unrealistic and that these kinds of activities only made the problems the industry was already facing worse.

Many people didn't like this, though. Accusations of snobbery were made against him, and Marina Fang of HuffPost made the point by mentioning Iger's large

pay deal when he returned to Disney.

THE PHILANTHROPIC PATH OF ROBERT IGER

Donating to the Mayor's Fund in LA

The Mayor of Los Angeles, Eric Garcetti, made an announcement regarding a significant donation made by Bob Iger, the Executive Chairman of Disney, and his wife, Willow Bay, who serves as the Dean of the USC Annenberg School for Communication and Journalism. The couple generously contributed $5 million to the Mayor's Fund for Los Angeles with the aim of providing support to 1,000 businesses in their struggle to endure the challenges posed by the COVID-19 pandemic.

During his COVID-19 briefing, Mayor Garcetti emphasized the crucial role of small businesses in Los Angeles, characterizing them as the vital force sustaining the city's economic and social fabric. He further acknowledged that the epidemic had resulted in the unfortunate closure of numerous enterprises, leading to significant disruptions within local neighborhoods.

According to Garcetti, the city allocated grants to mitigate the financial challenges faced by businesses on the verge of closure. However, due to the absence of federal funding, the waitlist for those grants accumulated. Mayor Garcetti expressed his pride in announcing that 1,000 businesses in the city, which had been severely impacted, would receive assistance, thanks to the substantial donation of $5 million from Willow Bay and Bob Iger.

The couple had previously donated a sum of $500,000 to the Mayor's Fund for Los Angeles at the onset of the outbreak. Garcetti expressed that the newly established commitment would assist businesses in enduring the challenges they faced, and conveyed deep appreciation for the brave leadership demonstrated by Iger and Bay. Garcetti additionally encouraged residents of Los Angeles to contribute to the fund, regardless of the amount, in order to have a positive impact on the well-being of individuals facing hardship in the city. Garcetti highlighted his familial ties to local enterprises, asserting that he is the descendant of two proprietors engaged in small-scale commerce, specifically a barber and a tailor. He further stated that his initial employment experiences encompassed assisting his grandfathers in various capacities, such as tidying up hair remnants at a barber establishment and participating in the sale of neckties at his grandfather's clothes store.

The Generous Donation to Children's Hospitals

Visitors at the Disneyland resort were pleasantly surprised by the presence of notable actors from the film Avengers: Endgame at a designated event, adding an extra element of excitement to their experience at the renowned amusement park. This occurrence took place on a Friday, when a special announcement was made by the aforementioned stars.

Chairman and CEO of the Walt Disney Company, Bob Iger, was joined by renowned actors Chris Hemsworth, Robert Downey Jr., Jeremy Renner, Scarlett Johansson, Brie Larson, and Paul Rudd in a commemorative event. The purpose of this gathering was to acknowledge and celebrate the generous contribution of over $5 million in monetary funds and toys to various nonprofit organizations that provided support to children afflicted with critical illnesses.

Notably, the Starlight Children's Foundation received a substantial cash donation of $1 million from Disney. During the official announcement, Iger declared that youngsters admitted to various children's hospitals nationwide will be provided with the latest Avengers toys at Disney California Adventure Park.

Enthusiastic admirers congregated along the pavement in anticipation of capturing a photograph with one of their beloved Avengers characters. Following the official declaration, the celebrities proceeded to engage with the young attendees by exchanging handshakes.

Following the ceremony, the celebrities engaged with children from the Boys & Girls Clubs of Anaheim and Garden Grove, participating in the evaluation of the newly released Avengers toy line. One of the children, clutching two bags of toys, conveyed his indescribable happiness. Furthermore, the children had the opportunity to interact with Larson, who offered embraces, took photographs, and distributed additional toys to the enthusiastic group.

A 10-year-old attendee named Tyler Yesenosky struggled to articulate his emotions, expressing his excitement and surprise at the unexpected turn of events. This charitable occasion aligns with The Walt Disney Company's philanthropic commitment, known as the Disney Team of Heroes.

Hemsworth, the actor who portrays the character "Thor" in the Marvel films, remarked that children worldwide, together with their families and siblings, who find themselves in challenging circumstances, serve as genuine heroes and a source of inspiration for him and his colleagues.

Brie Larson, the actress portraying "Captain Marvel," expressed that the presence of the children at the event served as a source of inspiration, as they embodied the qualities and characteristics of the characters portrayed by the actors on screen.

Supporting the Obama Foundation

The announced new contributors to the Obama Foundation encompassed the University of Chicago, as well as philanthropic organizations associated with esteemed film director Steven Spielberg and Disney CEO Robert Iger. This monetary contribution was the initial instance of a financial endowment bestowed upon the University of Chicago.

The institution made a significant contribution to the Obama Foundation, several years after spearheading efforts to secure the placement of the Obama Center in close proximity to its South Side campus. The charity reported a donation range of $100,001 to $250,000, while the actual amount donated did not exceed $200,000. According to a representative from the educational institution who provided a statement to the Sun-Times, the University of Chicago had committed to financially supporting a portion of the Obama Foundation's community engagement initiatives. This commitment entailed matching funds up to a maximum of $200,000. The University's support extended to various endeavors, including endeavors aimed at ensuring that the Obama Presidential Center generated extensive economic advantages for both the South Side and the wider Chicago area. The organization's headquarters are situated in a building located in Hyde Park, which has been generously supplied by the university at no cost.

The **Iger Bay Foundation** made a charitable contribution of no less than $1 million. Steven Spielberg has had a longstanding relationship with former President Barack Obama. The Wunderkinder Foundation provided financial contributions ranging from $10,000 to $100,000. Steven Spielberg attended the official unveiling ceremony of the portraits of former President Barack Obama and former First Lady Michelle Obama at the National Portrait Gallery in February. Steven Spielberg and his spouse, Kate Capshaw, were among the benefactors who contributed to the acquisition of the photographs. Illinois Tool Works, a philanthropic organization headquartered in Glenview, contributed a generous donation ranging from $250,001 to $500,000.

CONCLUSION

Robert Iger's historic career as the head of Disney has been much more than the leadership of one of the world's premier entertainment empires. During his tenure at Disney, Iger has been responsible for a wide range of initiatives. He has also highlighted the persistent obligation of business leaders to extend beyond boardrooms, genuinely connecting with communities, inspiring optimism, and championing transformations via his many charitable works, both personally and under the banner of Disney.

Professionally, the beneficent power of this man's vision has been seen directly in Los Angeles, which serves as the birthplace of many aspirations.

Personally, the kind gifts that he and his wife, Willow Bay, have made to the Mayor's Fund have thrown a lifeline to small enterprises who are struggling to overcome the huge difficulties brought on by the COVID-19 outbreak. These kinds of businesses, which are sometimes referred to as the "backbone" of the economy, owe a debt of gratitude to Iger and Bay since their charitable initiatives have protected them from the possibility of going bankrupt. The fact that Mayor Garcetti acknowledged this generosity, set against the background of federal financial constraints, presents a striking image of a couple devoted to the upliftment of the local community.

Another of Iger's affiliations with fundamental projects such as the Obama Foundation is just as crucial as its worth. He is actively investing in long-term ideals of prosperity and togetherness by sponsoring initiatives that seek to revitalize communities and stimulate intellectual and economic progress. These projects strive to achieve these goals by bringing people together. His dedication to a future in which education and community are interconnected foundations is underscored by his conviction in the need to cultivate centers of learning and cross-cultural discourse.

When all of these strands are brought together, it is clear that Robert Iger's legacy is braided with purpose-driven charitable giving. His accomplishments throughout his life serve as a model for modern leaders, illuminating the significant influence that can be achieved when weaving together commercial success with a sincere dedication to the betterment of society. When we consider the far-reaching effects of Iger's work, we are brought face to face with the sobering reality that genuine leadership goes well beyond profit margins and stock prices. Those things that leave an indelible imprint on the annals of time are the lives that are improved, the aspirations that are fulfilled, and the communities that are changed.